three hundred verses

three hundred verses
MUSINGS ON LIFE, LOVE AND RENUNCIATION

BHARTRIHARI

Translated from the Sanskrit
by A.N.D. HAKSAR

PENGUIN BOOKS

An imprint of Penguin Random House

PENGUIN BOOKS

USA | Canada | UK | Ireland | Australia
New Zealand | India | South Africa | China | Singapore

Penguin Books is part of the Penguin Random House group of companies
whose addresses can be found at global.penguinrandomhouse.com

Published by Penguin Random House India Pvt. Ltd
4th Floor, Capital Tower 1, MG Road,
Gurugram 122 002, Haryana, India

First published in Penguin Books by Penguin Random House India 2017

Copyright © A.N.D. Haksar 2017

10 9 8 7 6 5 4 3 2

ISBN 9780670090068

Typeset in Adobe Caslon Pro by Manipal Digital Systems, Manipal
Printed at Replika Press Pvt. Ltd, India

www.penguin.co.in

This is a legitimate digitally printed version of the book and therefore might not
have certain extra finishing on the cover.

P.M.S.

For my dear granddaughter
Freya
with all my love

Contents

Contents

Contents

Introduction

The *Shataka Trayam* or *Trishati* of Bhartrihari is among the best known and most quoted works of Sanskrit literature. The perennial interest it has attracted in India is evident from its many old manuscripts scattered across this country. The famous scholar D.D. Kosambi, who compiled its present critical edition, put their number as 3000, 'at a very conservative estimate'.[i] The many commentaries in Sanskrit and translations in other languages that have become available over time are testimony to the enduring popularity of the work.[ii] To quote its most recent scholarly translator: 'After the Bhagavad Gita, it is probably the most translated of Sanskrit texts'.[iii] This new translation into contemporary English, here presented, is the latest in a list that goes back almost a century and a half in time.

The work's usual Sanskrit name, as given above, literally means 'three centuries', and indicates the numbers in its three components, each consisting of a hundred verses.

All are *subhashita* or 'well said' poetic epigrams. While the mood and thought of each lyrical, gnomic and mnemonic stanza is complete in itself, thus making an independent impact, their overall themes form a triad, and the whole is presented in three separate *shataka*s, each with its own title.

The key words in these titles are *Niti*, *Shringara* and *Vairagya* respectively. They broadly reflect the politic, erotic and philosophic modes of thought and, in turn, focus on worldly life, pleasures in beauty, and a total abjuration of both. Some academics have also identified these elements with dharma, artha, kama and moksha—the four goals of human life in Indian thought.[iv] In the present translation they have been rendered in brief as Life, Love and Renunciation.

This work was described by its learned eighteenth-century Sanskrit commentator Ramachandra Budhendra as *vidyavilasam* or an 'elegant revel in knowledge'; the description underlines its poetic aspect.[v] The quality of Bhartrihari's poetry has also been lauded by respected scholars of the present times. According to A.B. Keith, this work offers 'brilliant poems in miniature, on which it would be hard to improve', and their 'effect on the mind is that of a perfect whole in which the parts coalesce by inner necessity'.[vi] To D.D. Kosambi, 'the crisp and polished stanzas' reveal 'a great poet . . . few can exceed the force of his epigrams . . . and the finality with which a sentiment is rounded'.

Many modern scholars have noted that this poetry manifests an inner tension and contradiction. The well-known Austrian Sanskritist M. Winternitz described this as an 'oscillation of the Indian mind between sensuousness and renunciation'.[vii] The American translator of these verses, Barbara Stoler Miller, remarked that they 'echo a tone of irony, skepticism and discontent', and 'reveal a lurking attachment to the world as well as a revulsion against its sordidness; there is an undercurrent of turmoil and disenchantment'.[viii] A more recent translator from Australia, Greg Bailey, while pointing to the 'tension between affirmation and rejection', added that the poet was 'not a cynic, but one who felt alienated from all social institutions', making 'his message very modern'.[ix] According to H.G. Coward, the academic from Canada who has also considered its psychological aspect, Bhartrihari's poetry includes 'both the sensuousness and sense-renouncing aspects of Indian consciousness'.[x]

These tensions have also been explained in social and ideological terms. Bhartrihari's modern compiler, Kosambi, was both an eminent scholar and an ideologue who dedicated his critical edition of these poems to the memory of Marx, Engels and Lenin. He saw them as 'a physiognomy of a whole class', and noted their 'acute observation of human nature' and 'distress experienced by a man of letters without some means of livelihood'. It is a 'poetry of frustration', he wrote, 'which provides at most an escape, but no solution', and the poet is 'unmistakably the Indian intellectual of his period, limited by caste and tradition in fields of activity', representing 'a cross-section of Indian intelligentsia of an age that has not yet passed away'.[xi]

Kosambi's view received an appropriate comment from his own erstwhile colleague at Harvard, Sanskritist D.H.H. Ingalls. In his review of the former's critical edition, Ingalls wrote that the perception in it 'explains the mood but does not explain the expression. Beethoven too was a hanger-on at rich men's houses, and singularly frustrated'. He added that 'the poetry of Bhartrihari remains beautiful and sometimes truly great'.[xii] As for the timeless human tensions it reflects, these would be clear to any reader of the present translation, though their underlying causes may be varied.

From the poetry one must now turn to the poet. As with many ancient writers in Sanskrit, there is little definite information about Bhartrihari. His dates, times and personal details still fall in the realm of speculation. Kosambi outlined four theories on the subject, derived from different traditions about the name.[xiii] According to one, he was an eminent Buddhist grammarian, also mentioned by the Chinese pilgrim I-Tsing, who alternated between ascetic and sensual life, and died about 650 CE. In another, he was a ruler of the Malava region, cited by the seventeenth-century Buddhist historian Taranatha from Tibet. In a third, he was a king who renounced the world and was recognized as a leading figure in the religious order named after the godly sage Gorakshanatha. This is also described in a popular song by the fifteenth-century poet-saint Kabir.[xiv] In this theory, as well as in the fourth—which describes him as the elder half-brother and predecessor of the legendary King Vikramaditya of Ujjain—he renounced the throne after discovering that his beloved wife was unfaithful to him.

The deep disenchantment this caused him is expressed in a well-known verse from the Kosambi compilation, included as the sixth in the Prologue of this translation.

Commenting on all these theories, Kosambi opined that there is nothing to prove that the poet was other than a learned man, hungry and in distress.[xv] However, the traditions of a disenchanted princely figure he has also mentioned still remain in consideration by other commentators.[xvi]

As for his dates, a recent study indicates 'the current consensus among scholars that Bhartrihari should be dated to 450–500 CE'.[xvii] Ingalls noted that the textual references to his name are older than those to the actual shatakas. The latter first appear in a Sanskrit work of 959 CE followed by another of 1304 CE.[xviii] As such, the present collection may have only assumed shape by the twelfth century CE. In the absence of conclusive information, the academic debate on such points may well carry on. Meanwhile Bhartrihari's poetry remains striking and enjoyable: it has even inspired a feature film and a novel in modern times.[xix]

This new translation endeavours to present the verses of the *Shataka Trayam* in contemporary language for modern-day readers. Their Sanskrit originals are drawn from Kosambi's definitive critical edition mentioned earlier. That savant stated that in preparing it he studied various versions as given in 377 different manuscripts, and noted in them a total of 852 individual stanzas. To identify the 300 originals as far as possible, he divided these verses into three groups: the first comprised 200 stanzas generally found in all versions; the second, 152 stanzas not found in all versions; and the third, 500 stray verses from only single versions. In the first group, moreover, vv. 8–76 were under the heading 'Niti', vv. 77–147 under 'Shringara', and vv. 148–200 under 'Vairagya', while vv. 1–8 of his compilation are not under any single heading. He also reproduced another 187 verses which he described as apocryphal and outside the compilation.

The present translation includes all 200 verses of Kosambi's first group, though their order has been altered slightly for better reading. To complete the totality of three centuries, other verses have been taken from the second and third groups, as also found in *Subhashita Trishati*, the eighteenth-century compilation by Ramachandra Budhendra that Kosambi considered 'about the best of its kind among those known'.[xx] Their placement in this edition is also generally in line with that in *Trishati*. In addition, some popular verses found in both Kosambi and Budhendra have been included in the Prologue of this translation and the Miscellany at its end.

Within each of the three main sections, sub-headings, mostly drawn from Budhendra, have been inserted for clarity. The bracketed numbers given at the end of each verse (right-hand bottom) are from the Kosambi compilation, added here for ready reference to the original text.

Translating the centuries of Bhartrihari has been a memorable experience for me. The verses are replete with succinct thoughts and sharp images. Their tone ranges from cynical to wishful, from erotic to didactic, from pensive to completely detached. Their expression is sometimes personal, at others all-embracing, and occasionally tongue-in-cheek. Their language is generally simple and clear. Some give vivid glimpses of the poet's personality. I have attempted to reflect all these qualities in free-verse form. Each stanza is self-contained, but can also be savoured in a sequence or in a group to suit the reader's taste.

Together, they form a rich anthology of poetry deserving to be widely known today. Like other such collections, this too can be enjoyed both through a quick dip and with a longer immersion. It is no wonder that it has been read so extensively and for so long.

In conclusion, my deep appreciation and thanks to the editors of this volume at Penguin Random House India: R. Sivapriya, with whom the work commenced; Ambar Sahil Chatterjee, who brought it to completion; and Shatarupa Ghoshal for its copy-editing. I further thank Sufian Ahmed, librarian at Sahitya Akademi, New Delhi, and his colleague S. Padmanabhan, for their assistance in accessing the principal research material, as also Shafali Bhatt of India International Centre library for her kind cooperation. My gratitude also to two old friends: Ranjit Mathur, for kindly reading and commenting on the opening section of the present translation; and Ravi Shanker, who presented to me two decades ago his own fine renditions of Bhartrihari, together with one in elegant Urdu sent through him for me by its distinguished author Imtiazuddin Khan.[xxi]

The present translation was begun last spring in Delhi, and continued during our summer travels at the homes of my son Vikram and daughter-in-law Annika, and of my daughter Sharada, where the first draft was completed. To all of them, my love and gratitude, especially for their crucial help with computers. As always I am deeply grateful to my wife Priti for her patient support throughout. This book is dedicated to our charming granddaughter Freya, for her forthcoming birthday on 8 December. She also has a fine flair for writing, and it is my fond hope that these ancient verses with their striking modern resonance may perhaps provide some inspiration through a glimpse of the cultural treasures that are a part of her heritage.

New Delhi   A.N.D.H.
August 2017

Prologue

1

I bow to that radiance,
peaceful and still,
endless, unbounded
by space and time,
which is the spirit,
and only known
through self-awareness.   *(256)*

2

From the taking of life, abstain;
from stealing others' wealth, refrain;
speak the truth; perform charity
in time, as much as it can be;
be silent, and don't tattle to
others about what maidens do;
of your cravings, block the flow;
to elders, all due courtesy show;
have compassion for all creatures
equally. Thus say the scriptures:
the faultless pathway to be this,
to excellence and also bliss.   *(3)*

3

Experts may deride them
or praise them to the sky,
glory may crown them
or merely pass them by,
death may be an age in coming
or strike this very day:
the good will not hesitate from stepping
on the righteous way.   *(265)*

4

One who does not know the pleasure
of art and music, or of literature,
is a veritable beast
lacking tail and horns at least,
and if midst men he goes about,
it's the animals' good luck, there is no doubt.   *(796)*

5

Is this on our side, or another's?
Thus do the small-minded see.
For people who are large of heart,
the world itself is a family.   (376)

6

I have always longed for her,
but she does reject me,
indeed she wants another man
who chases someone else,
a maid who is to me attracted:
a curse on her and on that man,
on the other girl, on Love, on me.   *(311)*

7

A scrawny cur, one-eyed and lame,
with bitten ears and tattered tail,
old and starving, covered with sores
maggot-filled, from which pus pours,
its foot stuck in a broken potsherd—
yet this dog a bitch pursues.
Even the stricken, Kama screws.   (2)

8

In times past, we both believed
that you were me and I was you;
what has happened now, by which
I am I and you are you?   *(312)*

9

There are divisions in this world:
one wanders in it with indifference,
one through means and modes of life,
and one delights in beauty's pleasure.   *(331)*

10

The lords tainted by arrogance
the learned struck by envy,
the rest are filled with ignorance:
these verses wither within me.   *(4)*

I

Niti Shataka

A Century of Verses on Life

On Fools

1

To please the witless is easy,
and easier still the wise,
but even gods cannot placate
one puffed up with a little knowledge.   *(8)*

2

A gem one may tear out
from the jaws of a shark;
cross even an ocean
with its tossing waves;
a serpent place upon one's head,
as if it were a flower;
but one can never propitiate
a fool with fixed ideas. *(9)*

3

For concealing ignorance
the Creator has devised
something very useful
and in one's own hand:
silence is the best adornment,
for people who know nothing,
especially in the company
of those who know it all.   (68)

4

Grind it hard, and you may yet
extract some oil from sand;
a person mad with thirst may get
water from a mirage; and
one may find the rabbit's horn
if it is in his fate;
but none can ever satisfy
a fool who's obdurate.

(319)

5

It is possible to keep in check
fire with water;
the sun's heat with shade;
with sharp goads an elephant,
cows and asses with sticks' aid;
illness with suitable medicine,
and poison with some spells.
A cure for everything there is
prescribed in the books that be:
however, for a fool,
there is no remedy. *(759)*

6

When I knew just a little,
my mind was full of arrogance,
thinking I knew all;
like a rutting elephant
was I blinded with pride.
Then, coming into contact
with wise men gradually,
my pomp and fever did decrease,
knowing myself a fool to be.   (5)

7

Not bothered at seeing nearby
even the lord of all the gods,
a dog does chew, with great delight,
a stinky, putrid, fleshless bone,
wet with spittle, insect-laden,
as if its taste is matchless.
A wretch cannot ever assess
the lack of worth in what he has. *(30)*

8

Better roam with forest creatures
in hills distant, hard to reach,
than with fools associate
even in the halls of paradise.   *(320)*

9

A rogue elephant he tries to curb
with tendrils on a lotus stem,
to pierce through a diamond with
petals of silk-cotton flowers,
to sweeten the saltwater sea
with a single drop of honey—
he who wants to lead the foolish
to good ways with ambrosial words.   *(67)*

10

From heaven to the blessed head
of Pashupati, the lord of creatures,
thence upon the mountain peak,
and on to the earth and the sea beyond,
thus is the Ganga seen,
step by step, always descending:
the fall of those with no discrimination,
also has a hundred ways.   *(334)*

The Knowledgeable

11

Knowledge is man's greatest beauty,
his hidden and secret wealth;
it gives pleasure, fame and comfort,
and is the foremost of all teachers.
In foreign lands it is a friend,
and is in truth celestial,
valued more by kings than wealth;
without it, man is but a beast. *(70)*

12

It is a constant source of joy
that thieves can never steal;
given away to other seekers,
it grows and blossoms even more;
it is an internal treasure
that goes by the name of knowledge,
that perishes not, at time's end even.
Kings, do not be haughty with
those who have it, for who can
ever rival them?   (15)

13

Where is the need of armour
for people with forbearance,
of enemies for angry folk,
of fire if kinsmen exist,
of salves divine if one has friends,
of snakes when there are evil men,
of wealth if there is faultless learning,
of ornaments with modesty,
and what is royal government,
if there is good poetry?   *(237)*

14

When wise poets, famed for knowledge
worth passing on to all disciples,
and their speech embellished by
the beautiful words of scriptures,
live moneyless in a king's domain,
it shows the ruler's folly,
for they are lords, even though poor;
it is appraisers who are condemned,
not the gems they undervalue.   *(13)*

15

Rings do not decorate a person,
nor garlands radiant as the moon,
or pomades put on after bathing,
or flowers that bedeck the hair;
speech alone a man embellishes,
when cultured and refined,
for all adornments fade away;
speech is the one true ornament. *(76)*

16

All hail to master poets,
skilled blenders of sentiment:
with their bodies made of fame,
they have no fear of age or death. *(55)*

17

Kindness to kinsmen;
and mercy to servants;
with the wicked, guile always;
and affection for good people;
discretion with rulers;
directness with scholars;
patience with elders;
valour against enemies;
and, with women, boldness:
by men skilful in these arts,
the world is held in place.   *(71)*

18

The swan does live in harmony
amidst a bed of water lilies—
that a riled Creator can
destroy, but not the bird's
skill in parting milk from water:
that fame he cannot take away.   *(38)*

19

It clears the mind of dullness,
with truth nourishes speech,
elevates the thought process
and from it drives out sin;
it blesses personal consciousness,
spreads one's fame in all directions.
Say, what wise company cannot
do for any man? *(42)*

20

An elephant, its temples dark
with fresh streaks of rut, cannot
be shooed away with a lotus stalk.
Do not disparage persons wise,
those who know the meanings true:
wealth for them is no more than
a bit of straw, with no temptation.   *(16)*

Honour and Valour

21

Just as the shining sun does spread
its light upon the earth entire,
so too can the earth be at the feet
of a single valiant warrior.   *(220)*

22

On its hoods, the serpent Sesha
bears the worlds which on them rest,
and on its back all this is held up
always by the tortoise king,
who too takes calm shelter in
the watery bosom of the ocean.
Oh! they are just limitless,
the glorious doings of the great.   (73)

23

Even though they too are present,
Jupiter and the other planets,
Rahu, valour incarnate,
has not their enemy become.
Brother, behold this king of demons,
now left only with his head,
eclipses, on appropriate dates,
just the bright ones, Sun and Moon.   *(53)*

24

Under the strikes of thunderbolts,
by Indra hurled so arrogantly
with such terrible flames of fire,
alas, it would have better been
for the snowy mountain's son
to give up life; but it was improper
for him to hide within the sea
when his father faced calamity.

(321)

25

The dog will wag its tail, and go
grovelling down, its belly show
before its feeder; but the brave
elephant gazes long and grave
at the hand which offers bread,
and must be coaxed before it's fed.   *(57)*

26

With hunger weak, by age worn out,
feeble, and in pained condition,
all sparkle gone, life at its end;
even so, the lion hankers
for a morsel torn out from the head
of a rutting, lordly elephant:
can this foremost of proud creatures
feed upon dry bits of grass?   *(17)*

27

Even a lion's little cub leaps
on to a rutting elephant's head,
it is not due to age or prowess:
such, indeed, is heroic nature.   *(75)*

28

Even with a bit of bone—
foul with scraps of gut and grease,
meat upon it having none
for its hunger to appease—
the dog is all the same content.
And the lion will, in turn,
in his grasp the jackal spurn,
and seek to slay an elephant.
In distress even, every creature
looks for food to match its nature.

(350)

29

Even a sunstone, insensate,
flames when trod on by the foot,
how can a man of honour bear
humiliation by another? (65)

30

With constant rounds to life decreed,
both birth and death are no surprises,
but truly born is one, indeed,
by whose birth the whole race rises.   (74)

On Wealth

31

One who has money
is considered well born,
learned, discerning,
well versed in scriptures,
an eloquent speaker,
and good-looking too:
all merits depend on gold. *(51)*

32

There are three paths for money,
donation, pleasure, going waste:
when neither given, nor enjoyed,
it follows the pathway third.   (50)

33

May the clan go straight to hell,
good qualities even further below,
from a mountain may character fall,
and lineage in a fire burn,
may honour be by thunder struck,
with us just let money stay,
without it all other virtues are
just bits of straw upon the way.   *(25)*

34

That for which one has been fated,
a little or a lot of wealth,
one finds even in the desert
and not more in the golden mountain;
so, be content, and from the rich
do not beg, it is no use:
water from both well and sea
fills pots by their capacity.   *(56)*

35

The gem polished on a whetstone,
the wounded victor of a battle,
an elephant quiet after rutting,
a river with dry banks in autumn,
the moon in final phase of waning,
the maiden worn out in lovemaking,
and men whose wealth is gone in alms—
all are splendid in depletion.   *(11)*

36

Someone starved seeks just a handful
of barley grains, but when full,
deems the world no more than grass,
such are the vagaries of wealth:
on its state, depending, great or little,
of things the value shrinks or swells.   *(12)*

37

The king is ruined by counsellors bad,
an ascetic by his company,
a child by being gorged and spoilt,
a priest by lack of learning,
the family by wicked offspring,
character by serving villains,
shame and modesty by drink,
husbandry by carelessness,
affection by living away,
friendship by absence of trust,
prosperity by policies bad,
and wealth by prodigality.   *(23)*

38

True and false, sweet-tongued and harsh,
merciful and cruel too,
tight-fisted but also generous,
extravagant yet acquisitive:
like a courtesan, the ruler's ways
do assume infinite forms.   *(59)*

39

Giving commands, attaining fame,
gift donation, luxury,
helping friends, looking after priests:
those devoid of these six interests,
why need they serve a king?   *(66)*

40

O King, as you wish to milk the cow,
your kingdom, then look after the calf,
the populace; when this is done
with due care, and constantly,
this earth will yield all kinds of fruit,
like a wish-fulfilling tree.   *(58)*

The Wicked

41

Lack of pity, endless quarrels,
coveting wealth or wives of others,
intolerance of kin and good folk:
such is the nature, well established,
of evil and wicked souls.   *(61)*

42

Keep away from a wicked person
though with learning ornamented;
a snake embellished with a gem,
can it still not be dangerous?   (27)

43

One is long to begin with,
but keeps on shrinking gradually;
the other continues to grow,
though it is small initially:
thus are the friendships of the wicked
and of people who are good,
different, like the shadows in
the morning and the afternoon.   (62)

44

No one can really be a friend
of rulers given to anger fierce;
touching the fire even burns
the priest who offers it oblations. *(60)*

45

The moon turned pale in daylight,
an amorous woman past her youth,
a lake bereft of lotus flowers,
the handsome visage of a fool,
a master with money obsessed,
a good man in dire condition,
and a villain in royal favour:
these seven situations rankle
like a barb within my heart. *(10)*

46

What need is there of other faults
if one is greedy and covetous?
Of other sins if there is malice?
Of penance when there is truth,
of pilgrimage when the mind is pure?
If there is knowledge, what of wealth?
Of allies if there is amity?
Of ornaments if there is glory,
and of death if there is infamy?   (37)

47

One modest is considered dull;
one who keeps to rules, a hypocrite;
in purity is seen deceit;
in bravery much cruelty;
a lack of sense in penitents;
in soft talk, servility;
one brilliant is described as vain;
one eloquent as too talkative;
and one quiet as impotent.
Indeed, is there a virtue, which
has not been slandered by the wicked?   (36)

48

Deer, fish and good people subsist
on grass and water, on being content;
hunters, fishermen and backbiters
are needless enemies of this earth.   *(32)*

49

Who can ever happy be
in the proximity of one who is
of virtues an enemy,
made prosperous by destiny,
and fruit forgotten of past lives,
who manifests every wickedness
now, with uncurbed villainous deeds?   *(69)*

50

A silent aide is dumb considered,
one good with words, a chatterbox,
one who stands too close is insolent,
and bashful, one who stays too far,
patience is thought pusillanimity,
intolerance, being impolite:
the rules of service are, indeed,
extremely hard to understand,
inscrutable even to yogis. *(35)*

The Good

51

Courage in calamity,
in good fortune, forgiveness,
eloquence in assembly,
in battle, valiant prowess,
for fame, the inclination,
to scriptures, devotion:
this is the well-known nature
of great souls and noble stature.   *(14)*

52

A yearning for good company,
of villains, full avoidance,
to elders, all humility,
to learning, due deference,
to the great god, devotion,
for one's own wife, affection,
fear of people's censure,
of self-control, the power:
in whom dwell such virtues pure,
those noble ones we do adore.

(43)

53

The hearts of good people are
flower-soft in prosperity,
but like a great rock on the mountain,
strong and hard in adversity.

(335)

54

As clusters of wild flowers do,
the high-minded have but courses two:
to be borne on every brow,
or perish on some forest bough.　　　　　*(34)*

55

They love justice in behaviour;
shun evil, even at the cost of life;
the wicked, they never supplicate;
or beg from one poor, though a friend;
in distress they are resolute;
and follow paths set by the great.
Who has good people taught to swear
such vows as swords' edges severe?   *(18)*

56

To keep one's gifting secret,
show visitors every courtesy,
to be silent when a favour doing,
but on receiving any help,
to speak about it publicly,
not to be puffed up with wealth,
of others talk with contumely.
Who has good people taught such rules,
like a razor's edge in severity?   (275)

57

Who would not in this world commend
the marvellous doings of good people?
In being humble, they rise high;
their merits are only known
in praising and extolling others;
their own interests are gained
in efforts made for others' sake;
and their forbearance
shuts wicked mouths, so full
of harsh and vile reproaches.   *(36)*

58

The hand is by donation graced,
the head by bows at the guru's feet,
the mouth in speaking truthfully,
the arms in matchless bravery,
and ears in listening to the scriptures:
good people are thus ornamented
even when they have no wealth.   (72)

59

That is a son, who pleases
parents with good conduct;
a spouse, who seeks the welfare,
in particular of her husband;
a friend, who does remain the same
in comfort and calamity:
all three are, in this world gained,
by doers of good deeds.   (279)

60

On an iron hot, a drop of water
evaporates without a trace;
but the same, on a lotus leaf,
glitters like a pearl;
and does become one if it falls
at proper time into a seashell.
Often, qualities can turn
base, middling or excellent,
in keeping with the company.   *(33)*

Helping Others

61

Trees bend down with weight of fruit,
clouds hang low when filled with rain,
with riches do good people bow.
Such indeed is the nature of
those given to helping others. *(63)*

62

An earring cannot grace the ear
as listening to the scriptures:
the hand is graced by charity,
not in being adorned with bracelets;
and kind folk shine in doing good,
not by using paste of sandalwood.   (54)

63

He diverts you from sinning,
and proffers good advice,
keeps your secrets guarded,
and makes the merits known,
in troubles does not abandon,
and helps when it is time.
Of a good friend, these are the signs,
as have said the sages.   (31)

64

The sun brings lotus banks to bloom,
the moon opens night lilies,
unasked, the cloud does water give.
The good do work for others' benefit.   *(64)*

65

When water is to it added,
milk gives it all its qualities;
and seeing milk come to the boil,
water too flows into the fire;
milk also, on its friend beholding
in the fire, wishes to follow it,
but is calmed with some more water.
Such is the friendship of the good.   *(28)*

66

Here sleeps Keshava, the god;
his foes too, the demon folk;
here are the mountains, given refuge;
as also the fire submarine;
and the clouds of doomsday.
How great is the ocean's fortitude
in enduring all this burden! (20)

67

How many are the saintly people,
whose thinking, speech and persons are
with such blessed nectar filled?
They please the world by giving help,
and their own hearts satisfy
by making into real mountains
the tiny grains of others' merits.   *(19)*

68

Cut down cravings, practice patience,
give up pride and sinful thoughts,
speak the truth, the virtuous follow,
be of service to the wise,
please even foes, respect the noble,
own merits cloak in modesty,
pity the distressed, guard one's good name:
such are the marks of saintly men.   *(44)*

69

Those are truly good men, who give up
their own to guard the interests of others;
common folk work for such interests only
if they do not their own oppose;
but there are fiends in human garb
who spoil others' interests for their own;
and those who do so for no cause,
them one cannot understand.   (221)

70

What of the hills, of gold and silver,
where trees too are no more than that?
The Malaya mountain we respect,
where trees, even with berries sour,
are found to be of sandalwood.   *(454)*

Character and Fortitude

71

Kindness embellishes a prince;
restraint in speech, a warrior;
calmness does knowledge adorn;
as humility, learning;
and gifts to those deserving wealth;
in rulers, it is tolerance;
in ascetics, the absence of anger;
in sacred rites, no artifice;
but the root of all this, character,
is the greatest ornament. *(41)*

72

For fear of some impediment,
the base will not begin a work;
the middling start, but stop as soon
as some hindrance does them irk;
but those of highest merit,
though struck by troubles constantly,
will not abandon even then
the task they commenced willingly.   *(277)*

73

The gods were not contented with
the gems the mighty ocean yielded,
nor did they succumb to fear
at the terrible poison it did spew,
their efforts did not cease till they
gained the nectar of immortality.
The steadfast do not stop until
the end decided is achieved.   *(52)*

74

Sometimes lying on bare earth,
at others on a couch reposing;
with a diet of just roots at times,
or of feasting on sweet rice;
dressed in rags, or robes celestial;
the steadfast one, on a task engaged,
does not think of pain or pleasure.   *(21)*

75

The tree grows even on being cut;
the waning moon does wax again:
thinking thus, good people are not
distressed in times of pain.   *(563)*

76

One whose mind is not transfixed
by the arrows of some beauty's glances,
nor scorched by flames of rage and anger,
or caught in the multiple noose of greed:
such a resolute one can gain
the three worlds in entirety.   *(230)*

77

Better that this body fall
off a towering mountain peak,
no matter how rugged, and
break upon the hard rocks below,
better the hand be thrust within
a serpent's mouth with its sharp fangs,
better jump into a fire, than
to let character be destroyed.   *(322)*

78

Flames then into water turn,
the sea into a tiny stream,
and a hill into little rock;
a lion then is as a fawn,
a snake like a floral garland
with venom, a drop of nectar:
for one, in whom character blossoms,
most dear to all the world.   *(324)*

79

Even when they are suppressed,
the steadfast cannot be debased:
the flame can never downwards burn,
even if the fire is upturned.   *(226)*

80

Sloth, which lives within the body,
is man's greatest enemy;
with which he can have no regret,
there is no friend like industry.   *(216)*

On Fate

81

A person bald, his pate on fire
with the rays of the noonday sun,
swiftly sought a cooler place,
beneath a tall wood-apple tree.
There a big fruit, falling down,
with a bang did crack his crown.
Often, one with fate adverse,
goes where there are troubles worse.

(39)

82

Brihaspati was his adviser,
his weaponry the thunderbolt,
his troops divine, heaven his fort,
Airavata was his elephant mount,
and the great god Hari favoured him.
Even with these marvellous strengths,
Indra was in war defeated.
Prowess is in vain, alas;
clearly fate is the one refuge.   (49)

83

A snake, confined within a basket,
lay coiled and starved, all hope abandoned,
when, at night, a mouse crept in
through a hole that it had bored,
and fell into that serpent's mouth.
By its flesh revived, the snake
escaped by that very mouse-made hole.
So, be at ease, it's fate alone
which ensures one's rise and fall.   *(26)*

84

That very rag of clouds which swathes
in the night the moon
does so too with the sun at morning:
O the wretchedness of both.   *(313)*

85

O the foolishness of fate:
while it has, in man, created
of all merits the repository,
a jewel to ornament the earth,
it has made his life momentary. *(342)*

86

This store of ambrosia,
this ornament of Shiva's crown,
this lord of all medicaments,
by scores of physicians adored—
but this moon too marks of illness bears:
Who can have relief when stuck
by the ways of destiny?   *(209)*

87

The reason is its mighty source.
That which in this world occurs
is as decreed by fate, the master:
even if the clouds may rain
every day and fulfil hopes,
just some tiny drops of water
fall into the mouths of *chataka* birds.   *(261)*

88

Like a ball when it is bounced,
the worthy, fallen, rise again;
but the base are like lumps of mud,
which fall and then fallen stay. (276)

89

O good soul, do not dissipate
your merits on futile pursuits.
To enjoy the fruit you seek,
propitiate that goddess, Fate:
she makes the virtuous wicked;
the learned, fools; foes, benevolent;
the obvious, instantly mysterious;
and turns nectar into poison.   *(29)*

90

Dear friend, a villainous destiny
whirls the wheel of a person's thoughts
with pushes of adversity,
our minds turned into balls of clay
rotated by a master potter:
we do not know what that will do.   *(278)*

On Action

91

We pay homage to the gods,
but they also submit to fate;
bow to fate, but it only gives
fruit to deeds commensurate.
If results depend on deeds,
what of fate or those immortals?
We must salute the act of doing,
where even fate cannot prevail.

(22)

92

In commencing any work,
virtuous or otherwise,
one clever will make every effort
to take care about results;
for the consequences of
actions performed hastily
can, till death, torment the heart,
not unlike a flaming dart.

(45)

93

In forests, or in battlefields
midst foes, in fire, or the water
of oceans deep, on mountain peaks,
while asleep, drunk, or in danger,
blessed deeds, done in the past,
guard and give protection.   *(46)*

94

The person who has in his past
done good deeds manifold—
for him a fearful forest turns
into a great metropolis:
all the people are his friends,
and the whole earth becomes
his treasury, filled with gems.   *(47)*

95

Good looks cannot give that result,
nor birth, character, even learning
and service rendered with much effort:
indeed, it is the fortune earned
from penances in the past
that for a person will bear fruit
in due season, like a tree. *(40)*

96

Those poor in words unpleasant,
but rich in loving speech,
not given to running down others,
and constant with their own wives:
by such folk is the earth adorned
only here and there.   *(206)*

97

One may into the ocean dive,
climb atop a mountain peak,
in battle, vanquish enemies,
learn trade, farming, all the arts,
and, making an effort supreme,
like a bird soar into the sky:
while what cannot will never be,
that which is, by doing done,
can it from happening be prevented? *(48)*

98

We salute that chain of action,
which makes the sun traverse the sky;
which made Brahma a potter
to mould the pot, this universe;
cast Vishnu into perils deep
of having ten incarnations;
and made Shiva beg for alms,
with a skull held in his hand.   *(285)*

99

Born on earth, this place of action,
the person who does no good deeds,
that luckless one is, as if, cooking
seed waste on a plate bejewelled
with sandalwood for fuel;
digging the ground with a golden spade
to get some roots of the common sun plant;
and, flavouring with chips of camphor
the barely edible *kodrava*'s roots.   *(343)*

100

A shining palace, lovely girls,
the parasol of radiant white:
one may experience for long
all these fruit of blessed deeds.
But when they end, this wealth does scatter
in all directions, one will see,
like a pearl string that is snapped
in the course of making love.   *(7)*

II

Shringara Shataka

A Century of Verses on Love

In Praise of Beauty

1

Salute that crocodile-bannered god,
Kama, whose amazing powers
cannot be in words described:
by whom Brahma, Vishnu, Shiva,
are into household servants turned
of goddesses with doe-like eyes.   (112)

2

With a soft smile, a modest manner,
a sidelong glance, face turned away,
with a jealous tiff and artful words—
women enchain one with such play. (79)

3

Clever raising of the brows,
sidelong looks from half-closed eyes,
tender words with hesitant laughter,
and gracefully to move and stand:
all these are women's ornaments,
and also their weaponry.   (92)

4

That maiden of beautiful brows
indeed has a faithful servant
in Kama of the crocodile flag
who prevails over every person
whom she signals with her eyes.   *(127)*

5

Sweet girl, what is this singular
archery that you display?
Not with arrows you pierce hearts,
but with the bowstring of your way.   *(133)*

6

With a face sparkling like the moonstone,
tresses dark as the great sapphire,
and ruby-red lotus hands,
she glows as if with gems embellished.   *(131)*

7

The pretty, darting eyes of girls,
sometimes under eyebrows raised,
at others lowered modestly,
sometimes timid and afraid,
or glittering in dalliance:
they are like lovely lotus blooms
spread in all directions.   (89)

8

They are like swans on lotus blossoms,
their bodies with saffron tinted,
garlands quivering on fair breasts,
tinkling bells around their ankles:
who on earth cannot these charmers
bring under their sway?   *(117)*

9

A lustrous face, just like the moon;
eyes that shame the blooming lotus;
the body's glow, more than of gold;
tresses dark, like a swarm of bees;
the bosom's curves, like an elephant's brow;
comely hips, voluptuous,
and a sweet, enchanting voice:
of young women, all these are
just natural adornments. (90)

10

A slight smile upon the face;
the warmth of a simple, liquid glance;
a flow of words, now flavoured with
a sense of some new luxury;
lithe movements like a tender sapling:
how charming is a doe-eyed girl
as she enters youth? *(93)*

Beautiful Women

11

A lamp there is, and fire too,
the moon and twinkling stars as well,
but without my fawn-eyed girl,
this world is plunged into darkness.   *(130)*

12

Breasts a burden great as Jupiter,
a face that glows just like the Moon,
the feet with Saturn's languid gait:
she is embellished by the planets.   *(132)*

13

Those poets have contrary minds
who always call a woman 'weak';
for women, with their flashing glances,
vanquish even Indra and the rest:
how can they be feeble thought? *(118)*

14

For lovers, what is the best of sights?
It is the sweetheart's blissful face.
Of scents, her breath; of sounds, her voice;
of tastes, the nectar of her lips;
of touch, her body; and to think about,
her youth and dalliance amorous.   *(107)*

15

The clink of bangles on their wrists,
the jingle of their girdle bells,
and the tinkling of their anklets:
these sounds surpass the coo of birds.
Which mind cannot these damsels
cause to lose every discipline
with their glances, like the doe's,
artless but seemingly scared.   *(80)*

16

Hair neatly braided, and large eyes
extending almost to the ears,
the mouth and teeth, both signalling,
a fully natural purity,
twin breasts swelling like elephant brows,
a resting place for lustrous pearls:
O slim maiden, though sedate and calm,
your form excites our passions.   (139)

17

Those breasts up-thrust, the flashing eyes
under rippling brows,
and the deep red of those bud-like lips
do unsettle me, of course,
though they are lucky signs inscribed
by the god of love himself:
but why does that faint line of hair
above her navel cause torment?   (119)

18

If her breasts are firm,
her hips enticing,
and her face so beautiful,
why, O mind, are you so troubled?
If you covet them, then earn merit;
without it they cannot be had.

(136)

19

Sweet and fond, intense in love,
with some touches of languor,
a joy to hear, so very artless,
by nature charming, and trustworthy,
but giving rise to sensuous thoughts:
by such words in private moments
from doe-eyed girls, who can't be won?   *(273)*

20

This glory of youth, this fresh scent
of girls with glances like the deer's,
attuned to a dalliance fierce,
a surety for gifts won in love
and of the mind's enchantment:
this age is rich with new emotions
and pursuits of luxury,
who can ever get over it?   *(217)*

Making Love

21

A slender maid in the forest roamed,
from time to time reclining
in the shadows of the trees,
her hands lifting up the dress
from her breasts to ward off moonbeams.   *(121)*

22

First, I simply wished to see her,
then sought the joy of just an embrace,
and with that pretty-eyed girl in my arms,
I crave for fusion of our bodies.   *(122)*

23

Blooming jasmine in her hair,
her body fragrant with a paste
of powdered sandal mixed with saffron;
with passion's languor, when that darling
lies upon my breast, it seems
the rest of heaven too is there.   *(116)*

24

At first, No! No! Then as a mood agreeable
forms, and desire does awaken
in a body, listless bashfully,
and resistance fades away,
with her limbs and legs stretched out,
a secret and much sought-after game,
skilled, dripping with passion, starts
with deeper pleasure: it is bliss
to lie with a good family woman.   *(124)*

25

Lying prone upon one's chest,
with her braided hair undone,
eyes now closed, now slightly opened,
the temples moist with the sweat
from the strain of vigorous love play:
of such a woman's lips, the honey
those who drink are lucky men.   (123)

26

That which does gratify
with the essence of lovemaking,
the woman who has shut her eyes,
is indeed the homage true
that a couple pays to Kama.   *(215)*

27

It is unfitting and untimely
for men to have erotic feelings
even when they have turned old,
while women too are not created
to love and lust outside the limits
of their bosoms drooping down.   *(128)*

28

No one in this world, O King,
has crossed the ocean of desire
or of great wealth. What is their use
with the body's youth and passion gone?
So, we stay at home, before the beauty
of our lovers with blue lily eyes
is by old age overcome
and swiftly made to disappear.   (86)

29

In this world there is no other
forest where so many flowers
of problem and disaster bloom:
it is youth—the abode of passion,
the cause of suffering terrible pains
in hundreds of hells;
the seed from which delusion springs,
a cloud which veils the moon of wisdom,
the sole ally of love's god, Kama—
in which manifest all kinds of sins.   *(106)*

30

Youth waters passion's tree, luxurious
with a flowing stream of amorous sport.
A dear ally of the god of love,
an ocean filled with pearls of cunning,
a moon to please the damsel's eyes,
it is a treasure house of fortune—
blessed is one who does not get
carried away in having it.   *(105)*

Some Other Thoughts

31

In this world, so vain and worthless,
how could those of mind untarnished
lose their steadiness, be confused
in the ignominy of service
at the palace gate of an evil king,
if lotus-eyed girls stood not there,
radiant as the rising moon,
tinkling girdles at their waists,
bent beneath the weight of breasts?   *(97)*

32

While crossing you, O World,
the other end would not be far away
if in between were no obstructions
by maids with intoxicating eyes. *(103)*

33

Be even-minded, give due thought,
gentlemen, say honestly,
whose curves are better enjoyed—
those of mighty mountains, or
of women aroused to ecstasy?   *(84)*

34

When there are, in the Himalayas,
trees rubbed against by Shiva's bull,
caves where holy sages dwell,
walls of rock by the Ganga washed,
and such sites of excellence,
which high-minded person would
demean himself in salutations,
if not stricken by women there
with fawn-like eyes and love's missiles?   *(341)*

35

Make your dwelling by the Ganga,
whose waters wash away all sins,
or between garlanded breasts
of a damsel who ensnares the mind.   *(135)*

36

What is the use of empty talk?
There are always two recourses
for men around this world:
women, young and handsome,
weighed down by their breasts,
and ardent with passion—
their wildness; or the wilderness.   *(85)*

37

In this vain and fleeting world
there are but two ways for the wise:
their time spent with the mind immersed
in the elixir of knowledge;
if not, then in caressing plump
secret parts of some young beauties
with hips and bosoms made for pleasure,
arousing them to greater passion.   (88)

38

Sensual pleasure may be worthless
or lead to troubles at the end,
and thus deserves to be condemned
as the seat of every fault;
but it has a certain power,
most strong and indescribable,
which does throb within the hearts
of even those with realized minds.

(83)

39

I take no sides, but speak the truth:
it is a fact, friends, in this world,
there is nothing more enticing than
a maiden with a beauteous bottom,
nor any which can cause such pain. *(81)*

40

Please the wild doe in the forest
with shoots of grass, cut off the ground
by stones shaped like a bamboo's knot,
or please your dear beloved bride
with a betel leaf of colours pale
as the cheek of a Saka maid,
pared off the vine with your own nails.   *(257)*

Love in Spring and Summer

41

With the sweet coos of koel birds,
and with a southern breeze, the spring
smites those separated from their lovers.
Alas, in their calamity,
even nectar will a poison be.   *(111)*

42

Languid after dalliance,
and filled with feelings multiple,
to be besides the sweetheart
in a bower of blooming vines,
with koels' love cries in the ears,
listening to good poetry
with glorious moonlight all around:
which heart would not be pleased by such
charming flower wreaths of spring?   (138)

43

When the scent of mango blossoms
spreads, causing all things to swoon,
and their sweet nectar maddens bees,
who will not be filled with longings?   *(340)*

44

A girlfriend's heart, it is well known,
may be resentful, but only till
the southern breeze is not filled
with the fragrance of sandal trees.   *(274)*

160

45

At this time does a koel look
longingly at mango trees
with budding blooms that stoke the fire
of loneliness in a traveller's wife,
its agony further enflamed
by breezes from the southern hills
scented with new trumpet flowers.   *(271)*

46

Breezes laden with fresh scents;
branches which carry new shoots;
drunken cries of birds which long
for their still-separated mates;
brides with glowing moonlike faces
and beads of sweat after lovemaking:
from where do these delights appear
with such richness in the summer? (99)

47

Moist with sandal scent, the hands
of maidens with eyes like the doe's,
homes with fountains, fragrant flowers,
soft breeze and moonlight on the terrace:
in summer all these do make intense
both passion as well as delight.   *(98)*

48

A house whitewashed and shining
in the clear light of the moon,
the lotus face of a woman beloved,
so fragrant with sandal paste
and a scented flower garland:
all these cause endless unrest
for a passionate man, but not
for one from pleasure turned away.

(134)

49

Well-fanned air, and moonlight,
a beautiful lake, sandalwood powder,
a garland of sweet-scented flowers,
lucent wine, nice house, fine garments,
and a damsel lotus-eyed:
doers of good deeds obtain
and enjoy these in the summer.   *(349)*

In the Rains and Winter

50

In the guise of a woman young
with the swelling breasts of clouds,
spreading the scent of nutmeg flowers
and turning on the lights of Kama—
whom do the rains not fill with joy? (141)

51

Dark clouds above
the sloping hills
where peacocks dance,
the ground below
all white with blossoms—
where can the traveller
rest his gaze?   *(87)*

52

The sky covered with clouds,
the ground with plantain trees,
the air full of *kadamba* fragrance,
and forests with the cries of peacocks:
all people, happy or unhappy,
are then filled with yearnings.   *(140)*

53

With flashing streaks of lightning,
such peals of thunder from the clouds,
such spreading scent of *ketaki* flowers,
and the peacocks' cries at play,
how will these girls with long eyelashes
spend their charged days of separation?   *(137)*

54

That darling girl with lovely eyes
cannot go outside the house
as it rains incessantly;
shivering with the cold, she clasps
her partner in a close embrace;
and the wind, cooled by the drizzle,
allays fatigue from their love play.
Even a foul day fair becomes
for those blessed to be with lovers.   (142)

55

Even needles cannot pierce it,
such is the darkness of the sky,
with thunder peals from clouds resounding
as rain pours down in endless streams
and golden streaks of lightning flash,
and women's paths to their lovers lead
to both fatigue and bliss.   *(212)*

56

Having spent in wild lovemaking,
with deep embraces and draughts of wine,
half the night on a terrace secluded,
one who does not, from the hands
of a sweetheart wearied with that sport,
drink water clear as autumn moonlight,
is indeed a cursed man.   *(143)*

57

At winter's onset, lucky people
dine on yogurt, milk and ghee,
dress in robes with madder dyed,
their bodies smeared with sandal paste,
and tired with lovemaking varied,
lie in comfort in their homes,
embraced by voluptuous women
with round hips and swelling breasts,
their mouths scented with betel leaves.
They indeed are blessed.   *(144)*

58

Like sensual rogues are winter winds:
they kiss the cheeks of lovely girls
and make them chatter with the cold,
their uncovered breasts they make to thrill
and swirl the garments off their hips,
giving shivers to their thighs. *(244)*

59

Often does the winter wind,
with girls behave just like a lover:
it shuts their eyes, their hair dishevels,
bent on pulling off their skirts,
hurt their lips with little bites
that make them thrill and faster move
with deep sighs repeatedly.   *(145)*

60

That which does not please one,
though beauteous, is never sought:
while the moon is so delightful,
the lotus does not care for it.   *(309)*

Blaming Love

61

To think of her gives fever,
to see her causes lunacy,
to touch her puts one in a swoon,
how can she my sweetheart be?   *(348)*

62

She is like nectar, only
as long as one may see her;
once she has passed out of sight,
it can be worse than poison.   *(125)*

63

There is no elixir nor venom,
leaving that girl aside:
in love she is a vine ambrosial;
averse, a creeper poisonous.   *(91)*

64

Only foolish hearts may throb
at the inborn charms of playful girls—
they are like the lily's natural pink
on which hover bees bewitched. *(82)*

65

Of uncertainties, this labyrinth,
the home of impropriety,
a city of audacious acts,
of sins and faults a repository;
this casket filled with all illusions,
the field of hundredfold deceits,
a barrier to the gates of heaven,
and an opening to hell's domain:
by whom indeed was it created,
this device, 'woman' called,
a nectar which is venomous,
a noose for all the world.   *(94)*

66

With one they will be bantering,
at one looking coquettishly,
in their hearts dwelling on yet another,
who indeed can a woman's love be?   (247)

67

Truly, never was the moon
their face, or blue lilies their two eyes,
nor of gold their limbs created.
But, even knowing this reality,
their thoughts being by poets duped,
foolish folk relish the bodies
of women, though they consist
merely of skin, bones and flesh.   *(108)*

68

This slender maiden's lotus face,
more lustrous than the full moon's orb,
with lips in which does honey dwell:
what of these? With passing time
they will like overripe fruit become
harsh, unpleasant, not unlike poison.   *(96)*

69

This river looks like your beloved,
its lilies match her radiant face,
its waves are like the triple fold
on her middle, and twin birds
soar up like her up-thrust breasts;
but if you wish to keep away
from its cruel, hidden flow beneath,
and sink inside this worldly sea,
then avoid it from afar.   *(101)*

70

As she is sweet, blue-lily-eyed,
with firm breasts, a comely bottom,
a lotus face and pretty brows,
even though he is aware
that she is a doll impure,
seeing her does madden him
to laud, enjoy, take her with pleasure.
Alas, the ways of infatuation!   *(231)*

Some Warnings

71

Their talk is filled with honey,
but their hearts have only poison;
so, taste the lips of damsels
but tightly press their breasts.   (298)

72

Beware, O friend! Keep far away
from that dangerous snake, which is a girl,
with a charming hood and a sidelong glance
bright as a poisonous flame.
For bitten by a common serpent
one may be with medicines cured,
but when it is by a clever lass,
the doctors too avoid one.   *(205)*

73

The fisherman with the crocodile flag
casts upon this worldly sea
the bait which is as 'woman' known,
to swiftly catch men as the fish
greedy for the flesh her lips,
and cook them then on the flames of passion.   *(114)*

74

In the forest of her body,
on the secret hills which are her breasts,
do not roam, O wandering mind:
there the bandit Kama lies in wait. *(104)*

75

It is better to get bitten by
a serpent dark as the lotus blue,
than to be by her glances pierced:
for snakebite healers are aplenty,
but, smitten by those pretty eyes,
there is neither doctor nor medicine.   (129)

76

The sound melodious of her song,
her beauty's sight, her luscious taste,
her perfume's scent, the touch of her breasts:
I swirl in these sensations five,
which seek their ends so cunningly,
that they veil reality.   (102)

77

Passion is a fit apoplectic
that attacks the human limbs,
its onset makes the eyes revolve
and sets the mind into a whirl.
By spells it is not curable,
nor by use of medication,
it cannot be set right, even
with the rites of pacification.   (126)

78

Can anyone be enamoured of
courtesans? They are like knives
that slice through discrimination's vine,
who submit their beautiful bodies
for trifling sums to rural nerds,
to the blind, the ugly and the base,
to those with limbs worn out by age
or infected with leprosy.   *(109)*

79

The prostitute is a flame of passion
fed with the fuel that is beauty,
in which lustful men do offer
their youth and their prosperity.   *(110)*

80

Which well-born man will ever kiss
a harlot's lips that, though charming,
are the cuspidors for spitting
by soldiers, gangsters, charlatans,
street performers, thieves and slaves?   *(229)*

Turning Away

81

They indeed are blessed, who
see damsels with sparkling eyes
and the arrogance of youth,
their breasts swelling, round and firm,
and the vines that are the triple folds
rippling on their slender bellies—
and yet whose minds stay unperturbed.   *(78)*

82

These languid looks from half-closed eyes,
O maiden, why do you cast on me?
Stop! Stop! Your efforts are in vain!
Now over is our age of youth
and its delusions all diminished,
we live in forests and regard
as no more than bits of straw
the net that is the world.   *(282)*

83

Gone are my delusions, and
the flames from Kama's darts put out.
But still that poor girl persists,
to incessantly look at me
with eyes which outdo blue lotus petals.
What could her intentions be?   *(218)*

84

O Kama, why take the trouble
of twanging your bow?
O koel, why this cooing soft
that you do in vain?
O pretty girl, enough of these
sidelong glances, sweet and smart.
My mind has kissed the feet
of the god crested by the moon,
and remains immersed within
the nectar of that meditation.   (317)

85

For those of minds joined with each other,
there is union even when separated.
But when hearts are split apart,
in union too there is separation.   *(328)*

86

A traveller sees the gathering clouds
and does not to his home return.
What is the point of going, if
that darling is no more alive?
And if she lives with someone else,
then too, go for what?   *(233)*

87

The lucid lamp of discrimination
lights up the learned only till
it is not extinguished by
the brightly twinkling glances of
pretty maids with doe-like eyes.   (77)

88

When the darkness that is passion
did cloud me with ignorance,
the world entire then appeared
as pervaded by that woman;
my eyes have now been favoured by
the salve of keener discrimination,
and a more perceptive vision
sees this whole universe as Brahman.   *(6)*

89

When their minds have been fine-tuned
by yoga's practice, and do shine
with a constant friendliness,
what need do those thus blessed have
of the prattle of some pleasing girls
with moonlike faces, honeyed lips,
scented sighs and shapely breasts
to be embraced while making love?   *(146)*

90

The pleasure from a woman is
no more than momentary,
and her breasts, adorned with garlands,
or round hips ringed with jewellery
do not give refuge from hell.
So, cease from it, O learned people!
Seek union with the bride of wisdom,
and with the maid, compassion, amity.   *(326)*

But It Is Not Easy

91

Renouncing attachments
are only words in lectures
in the mouths of learned pandits.
For who is able of forsake
the ruby girdles tinkling
on the hips of pretty-eyed girls?   *(147)*

92

He deceives himself and others,
that pandit, who does revile
young women so falsely.
For paradise, the fruit of penance,
is also full of nymphs.   *(120)*

93

There are warriors in this world
who can attack the rutting elephant,
some are even skilled in slaying
the fierce lion, king of beasts.
But those heroes, I tell forcefully,
are men rare who can suppress
the arrogance of Kama.   *(296)*

94

Man stays on the righteous path,
with modesty and courtesy,
and in control of all his senses,
only until his heart is struck
by the glances of amorous women,
that are like dark-feathered arrows
let loose from bows, their eyebrows
reaching back right to their ears.   (95)

95

Maddened with passion intense,
whatever women commence,
in hindering that even the deity
Brahma displays great timidity.   *(115)*

96

Majesty and erudition,
nobility and discrimination,
only last till a fire flames
within the body struck by Kama.   *(251)*

97

Even though well versed in scriptures,
in conduct, honest and straightforward,
and with a self-understanding deep,
rare are those who, in this world,
for a blessed state are qualified.
For with their brows can sultry eyes
turn the keys which do unlock
the gateway to the city of hell. *(100)*

98

Woman is the ultimate seal
of the crocodile-bannered god
for realizing all objectives,
and he is merciless to fools
who search for fruit illusory
and ignore woman in their stupor.
He condemns some of them to stay
naked, others to shaven heads,
still others to five pigtails or shaggy hair,
or the use of skulls as begging bowls.   *(113)*

99

Sages like Visvamitra, Parasara,
and others who did subsist
on air and water, eating leaves—
they too underwent delusion
at the sight of lovely women
with faces sweet as lotus blossoms.
Then what of men who do partake
of fine rice, yogurt, milk and ghee?
If they could control their senses
the hills would swim upon the sea!   (330)

100

There can be, the poet says,
one god: Keshava or Shiva;
one friend: a king or an ascetic;
one abode: a town or a forest;
and one bride: a beauty or a cave.   *(223)*

III

Vairagya Shataka

A Century of Verses on Renunciation

The Curse of Cravings

1

Hail god Hara, lamp of wisdom:
the crescent moon upon his head
is brilliant with its shooting rays
that blaze before their exaltation
to incinerate the moth that is Kama,
dispel the deep unending darkness
of delusion spread within,
and illumine the minds of yogis.   *(1)*

2

Through many inaccessible lands
I knocked about, but gained nothing.
Setting aside all family honour,
I engaged in fruitless service,
fed shamelessly in others' houses
with the greed of a common crow.
But, Craving, you want more of this,
and still are not satisfied.   (148)

3

In the hope of finding treasures
I dug the earth and crossed the sea,
smelted mineral ore in mountains,
pleased rulers with every effort
and spent nights in cemeteries
with mind focused on incantations;
but not even a single penny
was ever obtained by me:
O Craving, now go away.   *(149)*

4

With hopes of somehow pleasing them,
I bear the insults of many villains,
holding back the tears within me
and smiling with an empty heart,
my mind, by money stupefied.
O Hope, I even do beseech them
with folded hands, but you are futile:
why do you thus make me dance?   *(150)*

5

We do not enjoy pleasures,
we are by them consumed;
we do not practise austerity,
it brands us instead;
time does not pass,
it is we who are passing;
cravings do not wear away,
we only are worn out. (155)

6

For our lives, ephemeral
as water on the lotus leaf,
what sin makes us stoop so low
that, discarding discrimination,
before rich people, their minds
delirious with the wine of wealth,
we shamelessly do to them narrate
our personal merits, like a story?   *(168)*

7

The face is covered with wrinkles,
the head has gone all grey,
the limbs are slack and feeble,
only cravings youthful stay.   (156)

8

One's wish for pleasures has declined,
as has the respect given by others;
contemporaries, those dear as life,
have all now gone to heaven;
one gets up slowly, with a stick,
deep darkness covers the eyes;
but even then, this shameless body
is frightened of death.   *(153)*

9

We renounced all household comforts
but without contentment;
bore discomforts without forgiveness;
endured the insufferable pains
of the cold, the winds, the heat,
but did not practise penance;
we meditated day and night
with controlled breath, but on money,
not on Shambhu's feet;
our deeds were like what sages do,
but we do not have their fruit.   *(236)*

10

This life is like a river:
wishes are its waters, filled
with currents of cravings;
passions are the crocodiles;
and speculations, birds;
delusions are the whirlpools,
deep, so very dangerous;
and the steep banks are worries.
It drowns the tree called steadiness,
and those, pure-minded, who may cross it,
are exultant lords of yogis.   *(173)*

Dilemmas of Detachment

11

Though they may endure for long,
sense pleasures lapse inevitably.
What difference does it make if people
will not give them up willingly?
If they cease on their own, it causes
measureless anguish; but, renounced,
there is endless peace and felicity.   (157)

12

My food is what I get in alms,
that too tasteless, once a day;
my bed, the earth; my clothes in rags;
the bag, now with a hundred patches,
and just myself to be my servant:
but the hankering even then, alas,
for pleasures does not leave me.   *(158)*

13

The blessed live in mountain caves
in meditation on the supreme light,
birds nestle freely in their laps
and drink their tears of bliss;
but, in the mansions of our desires
on lake banks with pleasure gardens,
in festivities and playful sport,
our lives do waste away.   *(196)*

14

They do things most difficult,
those with minds that have been cleansed
by some knowledge of the Ultimate:
they renounce entirely
and with no regret at all
even wealth, which is the means
for enjoying pleasures.
As for us, we never had
any riches in the past
or now, nor surely in the future:
we only have a longing for it,
and that we can never give up.   (283)

15

I do not see as giving benefit
deeds which are presently performed;
on reflection, the fruit matured
of good works in the past accomplished
also raise within me fears,
for pleasures over time secured
by many meritorious deeds
are also, at their end, the source
of pain to those who love them.   *(263)*

16

Her twin breasts, just mounds of flesh,
are compared to cups of gold;
the face likened to the moon,
even though containing phlegm;
the loins, damp with trickles of urine,
are said to rival elephant trunks:
O how these despicable forms
are built up by clever poets!   *(159)*

17

Unaware of its fierce power,
the moth flies into a flame;
the fish too, due to ignorance,
swallows the baited hook;
and yet, knowing very well
this net is tangled with distress,
we do not give up our cravings—
alas, the denseness of delusion!   *(160)*

18

In lovers, Hara is singular:
of the loved one, half his body formed;
that is more than yogis, only freed
from contact with womenfolk.
As for the rest, who have been maddened
by the serpents poisonous
of Kama's unavoidable darts—
they stay caught in dilemmas,
in which they neither enjoy pleasures
nor are able to give them up.   *(224)*

19

One drinks water, sweet and cold,
when the mouth is parched with thirst;
eats rice garnished with meat and spices
when suffering from hunger;
and one's bride firmly embraces
when Kama's fire flames within:
all these, which people think are pleasures,
are only the means and methods
for treating an ailment.   *(253)*

20

A stately home and countless wealth,
sons by good people esteemed,
youth, and a sweetheart propitious—
thinking these to be eternal,
fools enter this prison, the world;
but knowing all this as transient,
the blessed do renounce it.   (252)

The Pity of Penury

21

If he did not see his wife
in that piteous state, abject,
her worn-out garments being pulled at
by hungry and howling children,
which high-minded person would,
for the sake of his starving belly,
utter the words 'please give', that stick
inside a choking throat for fear
that the plea will be refused?   *(152)*

22

It's better for one with self-respect,
when suffering hunger and in need
to fill the cave that is his belly,
to go into a holy town or forest
with a begging bowl concealed
behind a white garment,
from one to another door
dark with smoke from oblations
offered to the fire by
priests who know the laws.
Then he is blessed; not the wretch
who daily begs from kinsfolk.   (179)

23

Are there no edible roots in caves,
no waterfalls in mountains?
Have tree branches that provide
tasty fruit and bark for clothing
also disappeared,
that people look up to the faces
of villains who show no courtesy,
and with a bit of wealth, ill-gotten,
raise their eyebrows arrogantly?   *(184)*

24

Those boulder ridges Himalayan,
charming, cooled by Ganga's spray,
a resting place for demigods—
have they gone to hell, so that
to morsels, which others give with contempt,
men now addicted stay?   *(238)*

25

A moon for merit's lilies blooming,
also a vessel hard to fill,
this belly does shred self-respect:
like an axe that can cut down
a full and flourishing vine of shame:
it causes many dilemmas. *(207)*

26

Friend, content your dear self with
flowers, fruit and edible roots,
the earth as bed, new bark as clothing.
We shall go to a forest now
where no one even hears the name
of wicked minds immersed in folly,
lords with voices always marked
by the malady of wealth.   *(181)*

27

The days that kept on getting longer
with painful pleas before the rich,
and those that seemed to be so brief
when the mind was sunk in pleasure:
I do now recall them with
a laughter that within me spreads
as, seated in a mountain cave,
I come out of meditation.   *(174)*

28

In every forest there are trees
full of fruit that can be plucked
at one's wish and painlessly;
at many places there are rivers
blessed with water cool and sweet;
and a bed of freshly sprouted vines
has a feel so very soft;
yet, even then wretches put up
with torment at rich people's doors.   *(281)*

29

To live on alms is not debasing
in Shambhu's worship, yogis say:
it churns out fears and jealousies,
destroys pain and arrogance,
is easy to practise anywhere,
each day, and is dear to saints,
as a treasure pure, eternal.   (290)

30

Those delighting in contentment,
need no other happiness;
and those whose thinking is absorbed
in wealth, are filled with cravings.
If, whatever has been done
is by fate, then what is wealth?
I do not want the golden mountain,
my craving for it has ended.   *(314)*

Transience of Pleasure

31

In pleasure there is fear of sickness,
in family status of decline,
in wealth of kings, in strength of foes,
in prestige of indigence,
of age in beauty, and villains in virtue,
in scholarship of disputants,
and in the body of death itself:
on this earth, all things are linked
for mankind, to fear, except
renunciation, which has no qualms.   *(294)*

32

Birth carries the smell of death,
sparkling youth of old age,
contentment of a wish for wealth,
a happy calm of amorous
advances by flirtatious women,
merits breed public jealousy,
forest floors breed snakes,
rulers are with villains joined,
and opulence with transience:
what indeed is not possessed
or stricken by something else?   (197)

33

Health is troubled throughout life
by sickness, bodily and of the mind;
wherever prosperity appears,
doors open too for misfortunes;
one born will soon and certainly
be faced with death and helplessness;
thus, what is there which wilful fate
has made to last forever?   *(198)*

34

Pleasures are all fleeting, like
lightning streaks midst spreading clouds;
and life is but momentary,
like a drop of water on
a lotus leaf ruffled by wind;
youthful urges too are fickle:
and the wise, observing all this,
quickly do their minds apply
with steadfastness to meditation
through which, it is established,
yoga is attained with ease.   *(178)*

35

Life is fleeting, like a wave;
youth's splendour also lasts
only for some days;
wealth is just imagination;
and fulfilment of pleasures is
like lightning flashes in the rain;
the embrace by a sweetheart too,
though deep, is not long-lasting:
of such fears the world is a sea,
to cross which the mind should be
to Brahman dedicated.   (192)

36

Pleasures last no longer than
the crashing of a risen wave;
the days of youth's delight are few;
love for loved ones also passes;
life too lasts for but a moment:
thus, knowing that this world entire
is worthless, wise folk should devote
their minds to doing good to people.   *(293)*

37

Like a tigress, old age does
crouch before and threaten one;
illnesses attack the body
like so many enemies;
life too is trickling out
like water from a splintered jar:
it is strange that, even then,
people do what is not good.   *(332)*

38

You stay confined, within the womb,
painfully, midst excrements;
in youth you suffer woes severe
of separation from a sweetheart;
in old age even, you have women
laughing at you scornfully:
Speak, O men, if in this world
you have even a bit of comfort.   *(199)*

39

Why, O people, do you make
such efforts, wandering in this world?
It has pleasures of many kinds,
but they are all momentary.
If in our words you can have faith,
relax this noose of a hundred hopes
and with a pure mind do concentrate
on shredding the wants within yourself.   *(292)*

40

Those pleasures, while enjoying which
Brahma and the other gods
are considered just bits of straw,
and the sovereignty of the triple world
also tasteless seems to be:
good people, love not those pleasures,
they are only fleeting,
there is but one delight supreme,
that can always be achieved. *(286)*

Force of Time

41

Alas, O friend, that king was great,
of chiefs a circle at his side,
with a royal council, moonlike beauties,
a growing multitude of princes,
and many bards singing his fame.
But it all has been made a memory,
by the power of time, to which we bow.   (169)

42

In a house with many people
there now lives but one;
and where there was a single soul,
are now many; but in the end
there will not even one remain.
Thus, rolling night and day as dice,
and moving pieces which are people,
Time and the goddess of Destruction
play on the board that is the world. *(171)*

43

With the sun's daily rise and setting,
life too shortens every day.
But, with so many things to do,
time's passage is not perceived;
nor is fear aroused, on seeing
birth, old age, mishaps and death;
for, having drunk the heady wine
of delusion, this world has
gone wild, become insane.   *(151)*

44

Night comes again, and then the day,
but knowing this, do senseless creatures
still run about as they did before,
repeating works done previously,
for things already sought and gained,
and condemned by everyone:
of our delusions,
we, alas, are never ashamed.   *(316)*

45

On the great god Ishvara's feet
we did not meditate properly
to cut through worldly bonds;
did not even acquire virtues
able to open heaven's doors;
nor did we embrace the breasts
and thighs of women, even in dreams;
we were only just the axe
slashing through our mother's youth.   *(154)*

46

I never acquired learning,
well honed and suitable
for silencing critics.
Neither did I spread my fame
to the sky with a rapier blade,
piercing heads of war elephants.
Nor did I in moonlight drink
nectar from the tender lips
of a pretty girl.
Alas, my youth passed fruitlessly—
like a lamp that burns
in an empty house.   *(195)*

47

Knowledge pure I did not master,
nor did wealth acquire,
neither with a mind devoted
did I serve my parents,
not even in dreams did I
embrace girls with tremulous eyes—
like a crow scrounging crumbs of others,
my time just passed away. *(175)*

48

Those from whom we have been born
have long since passed away;
those with whom we grew up
are also now but memories;
with every passing day,
like trees on flooded riverbanks,
we too wait to fall down.   *(170)*

49

The measured span of human life
is one hundred years;
of this half is lost to night,
and of the rest, a half
to childhood and old age;
the rest is spent in work and suchlike,
also illness, pains, separation.
Where can we creatures happiness find
when life is more inconstant than,
and fickle like, waves in water?   *(200)*

50

For an instant, having been a child,
for another, a pleasure-loving youth,
for a moment, without any wealth,
for another with all prosperity;
at the end of worldly life,
his limbs worn out, withered by age,
and his body covered in wrinkles,
like an actor, man returns
behind the curtain that is death.   *(235)*

Ascetic and King

51

You are a king, and I too am
exalted with wisdom received
from a guru, served and praised;
you are well known for wealth and prowess,
and poets spread my fame all over;
thus, the gap between us both
is not so very great:
if from me you turn the face away,
I also do not envy you.   *(163)*

52

You are a lord of treasuries,
I of language, treasurer of words;
you are a warrior, I am skilled
in all techniques of subduing
the fevered arrogance of debaters;
those blinded by wealth do serve you,
but they also wish to clear their minds
by listening to what I say:
if you have no regard for me,
O king, I have even less for you
as I go away.   (166)

53

We are here content with rags,
and you with your great affluence.
The satisfaction is the same,
it has no special difference.
Man indeed becomes a pauper
when his hankerings increase;
no one is rich or penniless
when the mind is at peace.   *(177)*

54

Fruit suffice as food for me,
and, for drinking, tasty water,
the earth's floor for lying down,
and tree bark for clothing.
But the impudence of wicked people,
all their senses gone haywire
with the wine of a little wealth—
that is what I cannot bear.   *(161)*

55

We live on alms, with space for clothing,
and sleep on this earth's floor;
what will we ever do
with those who great lords are?   *(210)*

56

Not dancers, singers, go-betweens,
or with minds confronting others,
nor girls bending with the weight of breasts:
why then are we present here,
in a king's assembly?   *(165)*

57

In the past, this world was generated
and held by blessed, noble hearts;
others then did conquer it,
but like straw gave it away.
Now its realms in all directions
are ruled by steadfast men;
so, what is this feverish pride
of those who control just some towns?　　　　　*(162)*

58

What great respect can rulers get
from a world that hundreds of them did leave
without even a moment's service?
And those who have become the lords
of even fractions of its parts,
they ought to feel despair, not joy
that they display like fools. *(164)*

59

This world is but a lump of earth
encircled by a line of water;
to win even small parts of it
kings undertake hundreds of wars.
Will these poor rulers, so niggardly,
give us something, will they not?
A curse on wretched men who seek
of wealth even a grain from them.   *(304)*

60

The moon divine also took birth,
one whose bright head got installed
as embellishment on the crest
of that great god, Kama's foe.
But now, afflicted by the fever
of unequalled arrogance,
are men whom people do salute
to seek support for their very lives. *(338)*

Addressing the Mind

61

O heart, why do you every day,
endure such terrible anguish
in gratifying others' minds
to procure some favours?
If you are pure, then from within,
the wish-granting gem's efficacy
will appear, and will that not
fulfil all that you seek?   (167)

62

In vain why wander here and there,
O mind? Do take some rest!
What happens does so on its own,
not in another way.
Do not dwell on what is past,
nor imagine what may be;
instead, now enjoy those pleasures
which, by themselves, come and flee.   *(267)*

63

End this toil for sensual pleasures;
there is a blessed, better path
for instant calming of all pain:
give up these fickle, flitting ways
in love for a world ephemeral,
and, dwelling in peaceful meditation,
O mind, now contented be.   *(180)*

64

Can one rely on waves or bubbles,
on river torrents, snakes or flames,
or lightning flashes, or on women?
O mind, purge out every delusion,
and dwell on the heavenly river's banks,
seek love for the god with the lunar crest. *(182)*

65

Before you singers, by your side
eloquent poets from the south,
and behind you the tinkling anklets
of women who wave the whisks;
if this is your wish, be a sybarite,
relish delights mundane;
if not, then O mind, swiftly
enter into deep meditation.   *(183)*

66

As we pass by doors of mansions
on the streets of holy Varanasi,
in the patched garb of mendicants,
seeking alms that may be dropped
in the bowl that is our hands,
do not think, O mind, even once
with reverence for transitory wealth—
it rests but in the royal gaze
and moves about like a courtesan.   *(245)*

67

If wealth that yields all one desires
is obtained, so what?
If the foot is placed upon the heads
of one's foes, so what?
If loved ones are embellished with
one's riches, so what?
If this body lasts an aeon,
even then, so what?   (186)

68

When one lives in a lonely forest,
free of the ills of other contacts,
with no attachment for the kinsfolk,
or agitations born of Kama,
of death, rebirth, no fear in the heart,
just devotion to the god Bhava:
Can there be renunciation
any greater than this?   *(187)*

69

If people are thoughtful, then
they seek Brahman, light supreme,
infinite, devoid of failings,
with whose compassion all the pleasures
of lordliness and the rest
are just quirks of wretched fools.   *(188)*

70

O mind, you are so restless!
You plunge into the netherworld,
and traverse the firmament,
wandering in all directions.
Yet, roaming thus, by mistake even,
you do not go within yourself
and remember Brahman, pure,
through whom salvation is attained?   *(189)*

Forever and Momentary

71

Why study the sacred texts,
revealed, remembered, and histories,
or elaborate dissertations,
and enter the maze of rituals
that provide a place in heaven?
These are like traders' gives and takes.
It is the absorption within
the bliss that is the inner self
that destroys worldly pains—
like the fire at the end of time.   *(191)*

72

While old age is distant still,
and the body healthy, free of illness,
and the strength of senses undisturbed,
only till then, knowing people
make great efforts for self-improvement:
What is the point of digging a well,
when the house already is on fire?   *(194)*

73

Should we stay by a holy river,
in austere penance engaged,
or take care, with every courtesy,
of a virtuous and generous wife,
or drink the medicines which are scriptures,
or the nectar of rich poetry?
With a life of but some moments,
people know not what to be.   *(172)*

74

Seeing the white hair on his head,
which are on a man the stains of old age,
young women avoid him from afar,
like a well of outcaste people
with its scattered bones. (323)

75

The body shrunk, unsteady movements,
a row of teeth decayed,
the sight decreased, increasing deafness
and an ever-drooling mouth;
the kinsmen disrespect one's words,
the wife does not listen to them.
Alas, the pains for men of old age—
the son even is a friend no more.   *(242)*

76

When the mighty mountain Meru falls,
struck by fire at the end of time,
the seas, abode of many sharks,
and other monsters, dry up too,
and the earth, though held up by its hills,
also rushes to its end.
What can one say of this body's flips,
like a baby elephant's ear tips?   (306)

77

Masters are so hard to please,
kings' minds are fitful like a horse's;
our thoughts are fixed upon high office,
with wishes so very substantial;
old age robs one of the body,
and death puts dear life to end;
than moral merit, nothing is better
in this world for the wise, O friend.   *(258)*

78

When one's prestige has declined,
and wealth has got depleted,
supplicants have turned away,
kinsfolk left are very few,
servants too have disappeared,
and youth has finished, bit by bit,
then only this is fit for the wise:
to live in a bower by a cave
washed by Ganga's waters pure
in some Himalayan vale.   *(303)*

79

Beams of moonlight, and a glade
in the forest strewn with shoots,
the joy of meeting some good people,
listening to tales and poetry,
and the face of one's beloved,
with angry teardrops sparkling—
all these are charming and delightful,
but not any more, when in the mind,
come thoughts that this is transient.   *(193)*

80

Were there no mansions for their stay,
no music or songs for them to hear,
nor the deep delights of making love?
But good men know all this as fleeting
like shadows cast by the flame of a lamp
flickering as moths hover round it:
and to the forest they all go. *(315)*

In Search of the Good

81

Though we have, O father, searched
this triple world from its origins,
no one has come before our sight
or within our hearing's range,
who could catch this elephant of
the mind drunk on its arrogance,
born of secret, deep desires,
and bind it with self-restraint.   *(176)*

82

That freedom to move about,
to eat without needing to beg,
to have of good folk the company,
listening to that which gives
but one result, tranquillity,
and the mind gradually withdrawn
with due thought from things external:
I do not know of what great penance
these happen as the consequence.   *(308)*

83

At one place, the play of lutes,
at another, howls and weeping;
somewhere, a learned gathering,
elsewhere, a drunken brawl;
here a woman beautiful,
there a body fully leprous;
I do not know if this our world
is nectar-like or poisonous.   *(470)*

84

In the good, knowledge destroys
arrogance, madness and the rest;
in others it is the cause
of the very same defects.
Just as a place of solitude
helps penitents seek release,
but for those sick with desires,
it causes them to further grow.   *(250)*

85

In the heart itself do wishes fade
as youth into old age passes,
merits too abort in the body,
with no one to discern them.
What to do as time slips by
and vengeful death comes swiftly close?
Know that from these pains no way is out
except at the feet of Kama's foe.   *(249)*

86

By the banks of the Ganga, river of heaven,
on land by brilliant moonlight bleached,
sitting at ease in the silent night,
but with grief for a world in pain,
when will we call out, 'Shiva! Shiva!'
and our eyes fill with tears of bliss?   *(347)*

87

Wealth is fleeting, as is life,
and youthful existence:
in this world, so transient,
just dharma is permanent.   *(495)*

88

My hands the cup, my clothes the sky,
alone, at peace, of longings free,
able to renounce this world,
when will I, O Shambhu, be?   *(185)*

89

When will I be in Varanasi,
by the banks of the Ganga, river immortal,
in just a loincloth, my hands held up,
beseeching, 'O lord of Gauri,
O Shambhu, be pleased with me,'
and pass my days like a blink of the eye?   *(227)*

90

Those who have lost everything,
their hearts now of self-pity full,
dwell on the reasons in this world
and the ways of destiny.
But we will, in some blessed forest
drenched in autumn moonlight,
pass the night, our thoughts upon
the feet of Hara, the sole refuge.   *(325)*

The Renunciant

91

Tattered in a hundred pieces
is the worn-out loincloth,
and the cloak also in the same condition;
but he is carefree, happily eats
of alms, sleeps in a grove or cemetery,
treats friends and enemies equally
with the utmost purity,
and meditates in solitude:
all passion and loose thought destroyed,
the yogi now lives blissfully.   *(234)*

92

The world is but an aggregation,
why should the wise be drawn to it?
The wriggling of a fish does not
cause a turbulence in the sea. *(284)*

93

The earth provides him with a bed,
his arms an ample pillow,
the sky a canopy
and the wind a fan agreeable;
his shining lamplight is the moon,
his beloved is detachment:
at ease and peace, the ascetic
sleeps like a sovereign king.   *(190)*

94

Mother Lakshmi, nymph of wealth,
give up your hopes about me
and look for someone else;
for we have no wish for pleasures
and what is a wishless one for you?
Now, in a pouch of tree leaves folded
and purified, we put our alms:
and this is how we wish to live. *(302)*

95

Living on alms, away from people,
for freedom always striving,
on a path devoid of give and take,
in clothing mean and worn out,
with no ego or arrogance,
and the sole wish to partake
of the bliss of tranquillity:
such an ascetic there may be!   *(289)*

96

Is he an outcaste, or reborn,
a shudra, or an ascetic,
an expert in discernment,
or a lord of yogis—what is he?
With such contrary arguments
tossed out by loquacious people,
true yogis are never angered,
and on their path do carry on
with a mind contented.   (243)

97

For serpents, the Creator made
a diet of air, obtained with ease
without recourse to violence;
for beasts, he laid young shoots and grass
to eat, and ground to sleep upon;
but for men, with wits to cross
the ocean of this worldly round,
were made such means of livelihood—
in securing which, men's virtues
are, one and all, destroyed.   *(352)*

98

On a rock Himalayan by the Ganga,
seated in the lotus pose,
and on Brahman meditating
in a state of yogic sleep:
will such delightful days come for me,
when aged deer, without any fear,
rub their limbs against my body?   *(239)*

99

The hand their pure cup, and the food,
alms always in their wanderings,
the clear horizon's spread their covering,
and the stretch of earth their bed;
their minds attuned to non-attachment,
in themselves they are content:
blessed are they, all baseness gone,
they now uproot their karma.   *(269)*

100

O earth my mother, father air,
comrade light, good kinsman water,
and brother sky—to all of you
I fold my hands in final homage:
your company gave me benefits
and spread wisdom pure within,
all illusions are now gone,
and I merge into the Ultimate.   (301)

Epilogue

A Miscellany

1

In life, this is the fruit of love:
two bodies with a single thought.
If, in the act of love, the mind
is elsewhere, it is like
the intercourse of corpses. *(225)*

2

Give, give your curses and abuses,
indeed, you have them in profusion;
not having them, we are unable
to reciprocate the same to you:
it is well known that in this world,
one can only give what one has,
none can give a rabbit's horn. *(255)*

3

If, by chance, this world became
totally without the lotus,
would the swan then peck in rubbish
for its food, just like a cock? *(307)*

4

A man with no wealth swiftly went
and spoke to a corpse in the cemetery:
'Get up, friend, bear for a moment,
this burden of poverty;
for I am tired, and want to have
the comfort you enjoy in death.'
But the corpse stayed silent for it knew
it was better to be dead than poor.   *(422)*

5

You do not gaze repeatedly
at the faces of rich people,
nor speak false words of flattery,
or listen to their arrogant voices
and run to them so hopefully;
when it is time, you eat soft grass,
and rest in slumber blissfully:
now, fawn, tell me where and how
did you your penance do?   (678)

6

Though people get fruit from their karma,
and their minds too are to it attuned,
even then, for the wise its proper
to always act with all due thought.   (228)

7

O you bird, O chataka,
friend, listen for just a moment
with a fully attentive mind:
in the sky are many clouds,
some can wet the earth with rain,
and some thunder but in vain,
do not before each one you see
say begging words of entreaty.   *(721)*

8

The father, courage; forgiveness, mother;
the wife, long-standing patience;
truth, the friend; compassion, sister;
and the brother, self-control;
his bed, the ground; his covering, space;
and wisdom's elixir, his food:
with such family, O comrade, say,
whom need the yogi fear?   (550)

9

In the words *chita*, a funeral pyre,
and *chinta*, mind's anxiety,
the difference lies in a dot of sound
as people may see;
but one burns bodies lifeless,
and one those that still living be.   *(496)*

Notes

The verses in this text are numbered in the left margin. As mentioned in the Introduction, the bracketed numbers at the bottom right of each verse are those from the original Sanskrit compilation used for this translation and are given here for the ready reference of interested readers.

Introduction

i.   D.D. Kosambi, *Bhartrhari Viracitah Satakatrayadi Sublhashitam Samgraha* (The epigrams attributed to Bhartrhari), for the first time collected and critically edited, Singhi Jain Series no. 23, Bombay, 1948. Reprinted, with a Foreword by Acharya Jinavijaya Muni (New Delhi: Munshiram Manohardas Publishers, 2000).

ii.   D.H.H. Ingalls, review of i above, *Harvard Journal of Asian Studies* 13, no. 1/2 (June 1950).

iii. Greg Bailey, *Love Lyrics by Amaru and Bhartrhari* (New York University Press, JJC Foundation, 2005). The earliest known English translation from Bhartrihari is by C.H. Tawney, *The Indian Antiquary* 4 (1875) and 5 (1876).

iv.   Barbara Stoler Miller, *Bhartrihari: Poems* (New York: Columbia University Press, 1967).

v.   N.R. Acharya (ed.), *Subhasita Trisati* of Bhartrihari, with the commentary of Ramachandra Budhendra (Varanasi: Chaukhambha Sanskrit Sansthan, 1987).

vi.   A.B. Keith, *A History of Sanskrit Literature* (London: Oxford University Press, 1920).

vii.   M. Winternitz, *History of Indian Literature*, vol. III (Delhi: Motilal Banarsidass Publishers, 1963).

viii.   Ref. note iv above.

ix.   Ref. note iii above.

x.   H.G. Coward, *Bhartrihari* (Boston: Twayne Publishers, 1976).

xi.   D.D. Kosambi, *Exasperating Essays* (Pune: 1986). Also ref. note i above.

xii.   Ref. note ii above.

xiii.   Ref. note i above.

xiv.   Ramkishor Sharma (ed.), *Kabir Granthavali* (Allahabad: Lok Bharati, 2002).

xv.   Ref. note i above.

xvi.   For example, Chaturvedi Dvarakaprasad Sharma, *Bhartrihari Shataka* (Allahabad: Bharatvani Press, 1947).

xvii.   Ref. note iii above.

xviii. Ref. note ii above.

xix.   The film by Pattu Iyer and K. Subramnyam, *Bharthruhari*, 1944; the novel by Sudhir Kakar, *The Devil Take Love* (New Delhi: Penguin, 2015).

xx.   Ref. note v above.

xxi.   Ravi Shanker, *Bhartrihari's Niti Shatakam* (1996) and *Vairagya and Shringara Shatakam* (2000), both Bharatiya Vidya Bhavan, Mumbai. Also, Imtiazuddin Khan, *Shair Azim Bhartrihari* (Lucknow: Urdu Akademi, 1953).

Prologue

1.   This verse is found as the first in several Sanskrit texts mentioned in the Introduction.
6.   In some old accounts this verse has been given as the first by Bhartrihari when he was disenchanted on discovering his wife's infidelity.

I. Niti Shataka—A Century of Verses on Life

4.   'The rabbit's horn' was a figure of speech, sometimes cited as an example of impossibility.
10.   A reference to the river's mythical descent from heaven to the god Shiva's head. Pashupati is another name for Shiva.
22.   These are the legendary supports on which this world is believed to rest.
23.   In legend, Rahu was a demon who sat with the gods when the nectar of immortality was being distributed to them by the great god Vishnu. Upon Rahu's denunciation by the Sun and the Moon, Vishnu cut off the demon's head. He now eclipses the Sun and the Moon from time to time in revenge.
24.   In a myth, when the god Indra was cutting off the wings of mountains to prevent their flying, Mount Mainaka, son of

Himalaya, hid in the sea to save himself. This is sometimes cited as an example of dishonourable behaviour.

66.   The ocean provided in legend a resting place for Vishnu, here called Keshava, and the others cited here.

73.   A reference to the sequence in which treasures appeared during the legendary churning of the ocean by gods and demons.

82.   In legend, Indra was the king of heaven, the sage Brihaspati his adviser and Vishnu (or Hari) the protector.

86.   Mythical attributes of the Moon.

87.   In legend, the *chataka* bird only quenched its thirst by drinking the raindrops falling from a cloud.

98.   Brahma is the Hindu god of creation.

99.   *Kodrava* is species of grain only the poorest people ate.

II. Shringara Shataka—A Century of Verses on Love

1.   The fourth line names the three great gods of the Hindu trinity.

2.   This verse plays on the double meaning of the Sanskrit word *guna* which stands for a bowstring as well as a quality.

13.   See Niti 82.

26.   Kama is the god of love and desire.

34.   The god Shiva's mount is traditionally a great bull.

40.   The Shaka, a name also found in other works, was of a people from the extreme north.

52.   *Kadamba,* also called the bur-flower, is a tree with fragrant flowers which bloom in the rains.

58. *Ketaki* (or *Pandanua odoratissimus*), common name keora, is also a medicinal shrub known for its fragrance.

73. The reference is to the god mentioned in 26 above, whose crest features a crocodile. Also in 1 above.

84. This refers to the god Shiva as in 1 above.

88. The divine infinite in ancient Indian philosophy.

95. The god of creation, see 1 above.

98. A cynical reference to the attires of various types of roaming ascetics.

99. This refers to the legendary seduction of two famous sages in an ancient Indian tradition.

100. Keshava is another name for the god Vishnu (see 1 above). He and Shiva were the two main gods popularly worshipped at the time, as they are to this day.

III. Vairagya Shataka—A Century of Verses on Renunciation

1. Hara is another name for the great god Shiva mentioned in Shringara 1. Others used here are: Shambhu, Ishvara, Bhava and moon-crested, in verses marked below.

9. See 1 above.

14. The third line here is a translation of the Sanskrit *brhamajnana.*

45. See 1 above.

60. The god mentioned is Shiva, but the legend is unclear.

61. The reference is to *chintamani,* a mythical gem that granted wishes.

64. See 1 above.

68. See 1 above.

71. The second and third lines refer to ancient scriptures called Veda, Smriti, Purana and Shastra.
87. The word dharma has multiple meanings, here broadly indicating the righteous way.
88. See 1 above.
89. See 1 above.
90. See 1 above.
96. The reference here is to the traditional Hindu varna system of four castes. Those born in the first three were entitled to ritual rebirth in present life, but not Shudra, the lowest. Outside this system were outcastes, considered even lower, and also ascetics who renounced the world.
98. This refers to the yogic posture padmasana often used in meditation.
99. The underlying concept envisages results in the present life of actions performed in past lives, which may then be converted into other actions.

Epilogue: A Miscellany

2. See also Niti 1, for 'rabbit's horn'.
6. See also Vairagya 99 for karma.

Bibliography

Sanskrit Texts

Acharya, N.R., with Kosambi, D.D., (ed.), *Bhatrhari Viracitam Satakatrayam* with commentary by Ramachandra Budhendra, Varanasi: Chaukhamba Sanskrit Sansthan, 1987.

Kosambi, D.D. (ed.), *Bhartrhari Viracitah Satakatrayadi Sublhashitam Samgraha* (The epigrams attributed to Bhartrhari), Singhi Jain Series no. 23, Bombay: 1948 and New Delhi: Munshiram Manoharlal Publishers, 2000.

Vyas, M.C. and Pathak R.C., (eds), *Bhartrhari Viracitam Satakatrayam,* Gayaghat, Benaras: Bhagavan Publishers, 1951.

Translations into English

Brough, John, (tr. of selected verses) *Poems from the Sanskrit,* Penguin Classics, 1968.

Miller, Barbara Stoler, (tr. with Sanskrit transliteration) *Bhartrihari's Poems,* New York: Columbia University Press, 1967.

Ryder, A.W., (tr. of selected verses) *Women's Eyes,* San Francisco: 1910.

Sri Aurobindo, (tr. only from Niti Shataka) *Century of Life* and *The Translations*, Pondicherry: Sri Aurobindo Ashram Trust.

Swami Vivekananda, (tr. only from Vairagya Shataka), *In Search of God and Other Poems*, Mayavati: Advaita Ashrama, 1968.

Warder, B.H. (tr.), *The Satakas of Bhartrihari*, London: 1886.

Also see notes to the Introduction.

Other Works

Chattopadhyaya, B. (ed.), *Combined Methods in Indology* (containing an essay on 'The Quality of Renunciation in Bhartrhari's Poetry' by D.D. Kosambi), New Delhi: Oxford University Press.

Coward, H.G., *Bhartrhari*, Boston: Twayne Publications, 1976.

Ingalls, D.H.H., Review (The epigrams attributed to Bhartrhari), *Harvard Journal of Asiatic Studies*, 13 (1950).